The Fisherman's
Little Instruction Book

Also available from Thorsons

A Baby's Little Instruction Book
David Brawn

A Cat's Little Instruction Book
Leigh W. Rutledge

A Dog's Little Instruction Book
David Brawn

The Driver's Little Instruction Book
Mike Leonard

The Gardener's Little Instruction Book
Violet Wood

Life's Little Instruction Book
H. Jackson Brown Jr

Life's Little Instruction Book Volume II
H. Jackson Brown Jr

The Lovers' Little Instruction Book
Cindy Francis

The Office Life Little Instruction Book
Holly Budd

The Parent's Little Instruction Book
Cindy Francis

The Salesperson's Little Instruction Book
Sean McArthur

The Scot's Little Instruction Book
Tony Sweeney

A Teddy Bear's Little Instruction Book
David and Tracey Brawn

The Fisherman's
Little Instruction Book

Rod Rest

Thorsons
An Imprint of HarperCollins*Publishers*

Thorsons
An Imprint of HarperCollins*Publishers*
77–85 Fulham Palace Road
Hammersmith, London W6 8JB
1160 Battery Street
San Francisco, California 94111–1213

Published by Thorsons 1996
1 3 5 7 9 10 8 6 4 2

© Rod Rest 1996

Cartoons by Mike Gordon

Rod Rest asserts the moral right to
be identified as the author of this work

A catalogue record for this book
is available from the British Library

ISBN 0 7225 3267 9

Printed in Great Britain by
Caledonian International Book Manufacturing Ltd, Glasgow

For David Penniston,
my fishing companion of 25 years.
(And with thanks to Richard Webber.)

Introduction

Fishing, in my book, is a pastime. I really can't consider it a sport, any more than I can readily refer to it as 'angling'. It is also a passion, which is as much about enjoying the beauty of a quiet, still lake on a warm June morning or the unexpected appearance of a kingfisher as it is about watching a waggler slide beneath the water to signal the first catch of the day.

The little instructions in this book are based on 30 years of making mistakes and listening to others. I don't promise you'll catch more fish as a result of reading them, but they might help somewhere along the line.

Remember, you don't even have to catch fish to become a fisherman. An ability to exaggerate coupled with blind optimism will do.

Rod Rest, May 1996

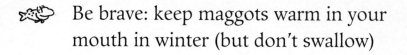 Be brave: keep maggots warm in your mouth in winter (but don't swallow)

Take advice from those older than you – fishing is 90 per cent experience...

...and 10 per cent luck

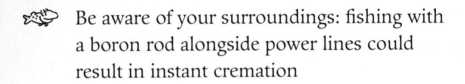

Be aware of your surroundings: fishing with a boron rod alongside power lines could result in instant cremation

Conform to type: concoct exaggerated stories about the one that got away

Think of others: if you plan to keep
a bait box of maggots in the fridge,
make sure the lid is on tightly

 Go fishing with an old friend. Even if you
catch nothing you can re-live past glories

Know the symptoms of Weil's Disease: if you're running a temperature and begin to feel nauseous following a fishing trip, go straight to hospital

 Be kind to fish: use barbless hooks

Be a self-appointed guardian of the countryside: clear away all litter (especially unwanted line) before you go home

 Report pollution to your local water authority

And for children:

Be safe – make sure they can swim
before they start fishing

Teach them during summer –
a freezing winter morning may
put them off for life

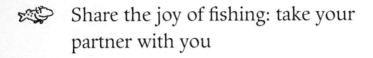 Share the joy of fishing: take your partner with you

Remember, boilies are for bait, *not* for lunch

Don't waste unused bait: give it to someone else before you go home

 Start fishing for tench, they're the most beautiful of fish

Always have one last cast (just in case...)

 Indulge in nostalgia – buy a copy of *Fishing with Mr. Crabtree* (But remember, you don't *have* to wear a suit and tie to go fishing.)

Be prudent: when you begin fishing don't buy more than three floats. After all, you'll probably only use one for the first few months – the one with which you catch your first fish

Learn to tie a good half-blood knot –
it will serve you well in most situations

 Stay calm: if you get a bird's nest,
cut and re-tie the line

 Be legal: buy a rod licence (or risk
confiscation of your rod)

Don't use a keep-net – return the fish to water immediately. This is not only kinder to the fish, but will also mean you've got a chance of catching it again

 Think ahead: if you go boat-fishing on a windy day, prepare your strategy for having a pee

If *you* catch a whopper, affect quiet modesty (punching the air and whooping with delight is bad form)

 If the guy on the opposite bank catches a whopper, go and ask him which bait he's using

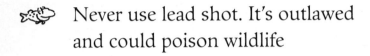 Never use lead shot. It's outlawed
and could poison wildlife

Remember, slamming your car door early
in the morning may wake the neighbours
(if that doesn't work, try sounding the horn)

If your companion catches a whopper,
say, 'It's a beauty'

Arrive on the bank an hour before daybreak. There will be enough light to tackle up and you'll be there to enjoy the sunrise

 Take time out to relax: a sunlounger is an essential accessory on summer afternoons

 Desist from naming fish after your relatives

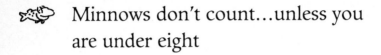 Minnows don't count…unless you are under eight

Invest in a good disgorger and always use it to unhook your fish

Don't silhouette yourself against the sky. Keep low or the fish will see you

Don't take a radio with you – it won't add to the day and might annoy fellow fishermen

 Don't be selfish: if you go fishing very early on a Saturday, don't expect your partner to allow you a lie-in on the Sunday (it's their weekend too)

Otters are fun to watch but they signal the end to your fishing

 Don't panic: a barbed hook embedded in your hand will usually come out if you wiggle it around for a few minutes (but if in doubt, visit out-patients)

When your companion goes for a pee, shout excitedly, 'Hey, you've got a bite!' By the time he's rushed back he will, of course, have 'missed' it. Expressions such as 'Oh, bad luck' or 'Never mind' will add to the authenticity of the moment

 A carp fanatic is a fisherman with bells on

Add flavour to your bait: carp go for tutti frutti, chub for molasses

 Express concern if someone casts their rod into the water (unless you deliberately want to humiliate them, in which case throw your head back, place hands on hips and roar with laughter)

- Be crude: make 'hilarious' jokes about your tackle

- Be scientific: don't guess the water's depth, use a plummet

- Remember, it's not the length of your rod, but what you do with it

A hook caught in reeds or on the bottom can normally be freed by laying down your rod and tugging with your hands on the line

 If someone falls into the water, be quite sure they're not drowning before you continue fishing

Always look behind before you cast

 Be prepared: tackle up the night before on freezing days

He who casts longest is a show-off

 Don't swear at the fish – it's not their fault that they don't want to get caught

Be still – a kingfisher might visit you

 If it's an early start and you're collecting a friend, phone him before you leave home to ensure that he's out of bed

 Think 'safety': tackle left across tow-paths can result in broken rods and furious, wet cyclists

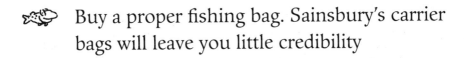 Buy a proper fishing bag. Sainsbury's carrier bags will leave you little credibility

Go easy on the hip flask or you might end up trying to smoke your hemp (or worse still, your worms)

Fish light on canals: one-pound line and a size 18 hook will serve you well for 80 per cent of anything you're likely to catch

 Use a landing net – it prevents your line from stretching

 Tickle trout...

 ...but don't try the same with pike

 Respect the close season where it applies

'Warm up' the fish: begin groundbaiting your favourite swim for three days before the season opens

 Be creative: make your own floats

If you want to catch tench:

> a) add sugar to your groundbait

> b) fish at first light in June

> c) try sweetcorn as bait

 If you catch an enormous fish, act cool and look like you do it all the time

Be adventurous: go night fishing in the summer

 Collect old reels. They're works of art and can be a great investment

 Take care of your eyes: a peaked cap and polarized sunglasses eliminate glare

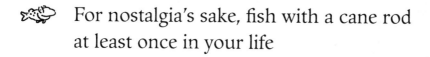 For nostalgia's sake, fish with a cane rod at least once in your life

Dye your bait different colours – it fools the fish

When fishing in a canal, ask the lock keeper about likely movement of boats

Wear drab clothes for camouflage

 Don't take your eyes off your float

 Fish alongside features such as bridges, moored boats or trees – fish use these as cover

Garden worms need larger hooks and need to be hooked through the body at least twice

 Take a camera with you – even if you don't catch a fish, the sunrise might be beautiful

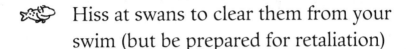 Hiss at swans to clear them from your swim (but be prepared for retaliation)

Quack at ducks...

...but mimicking fish will only make you look ridiculous

Don't be afraid to experiment: if the fish aren't biting, change bait, hook size, line, depth or your swim

 Learn to swim – it could save your life (but don't even contemplate arm-bands or a rubber ring)

Don't stomp around. Fish are sensitive
to vibration

 Use a waggler on stillwaters: they're perfect
bite indicators in this environment

 Relax

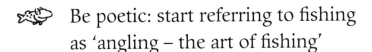 Be poetic: start referring to fishing as 'angling – the art of fishing'

Be brave: don't be intimidated by the large dog in the tackle shop

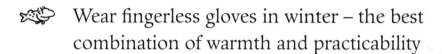 Wear fingerless gloves in winter – the best combination of warmth and practicability

Don't walk on frozen ponds – it could be fatal

Always read a fishery's rules and guidelines, noting *when* you can fish and the types of bait permitted

 Use a pole when fishing for roach: you'll get a faster strike for those quicksilver bites

Avoid fishing in *clear* stillwaters: fish can see you

 Learn how to position shot properly: this affects the speed at which the line sinks and the feel to the fish

Loading line:

> before you do this, wrap a rubber band
> around the spool to give it grip
>
> fill the spool to the edge – this makes
> casting easier

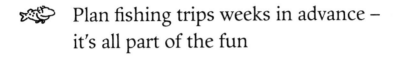 Plan fishing trips weeks in advance –
it's all part of the fun

Be patient: sometimes your only catch
comes at the very end of the day

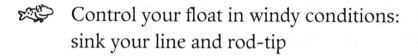 Control your float in windy conditions: sink your line and rod-tip

Save on tackle: cast underarm when fishing beneath trees

For winter:

    fish where the sun is on the water

    use maggots and casters for bait

For summer:

book a punt for a day's fishing on
the lake at Blenheim Palace – it's
a magnificent setting

If you've tried everything, have been fishing all morning and *still* aren't getting any bites, accept that playing 'Twenty Questions' might be the order of the day

 By all means use a spinner, but how many people do you actually know who regularly catch fish this way?

If you feel the need to take a portable TV with you to the riverbank, realize now that you're never going to make it as a serious fisherman (and on no account wear slippers)

 Fishing is not a metaphor for real life, merely a temporary escape

Never *throw* fish back. Gently submerge them and hold them lightly until they're ready to swim away

 Picking flowers from the countryside is not only damaging to the environment but they also make unconvincing bouquets for your partner

If you need to slip a shop-bought fish into your catch, ensure that it is appropriate to the venue. A tuna is an improbable catch in a canal

 Freeline on stillwater – this method can be lethal for surface feeders

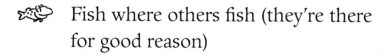 Fish where others fish (they're there for good reason)

Practise casting a fly on the local pond. Then practise and practise and practise

Fishing in ornamental ponds doesn't count

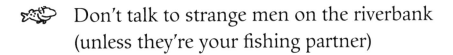 Don't talk to strange men on the riverbank
(unless they're your fishing partner)

If you catch a good fish, show it to a
youngster and point out the beauty of
its features

Be comfortable: always wear Wellington boots or waders

 But don't wear them if you're driving – they're cumbersome and could be dangerous

Ignore the holiday cottage sales pitch of 'You can practically fish from the window.' Have you tried casting with a 14-foot rod via a 3-foot high opening?

 Beware the fish's last gasp fight for freedom – it isn't yours until it's safely on the bank

Swot up on your baits – know the difference between a maggot and a caster, a pinkie and a gozzer

 If you're young and squeamish, take a grandparent with you to hook the baits. They've seen it all before. Plus they'd love to be asked

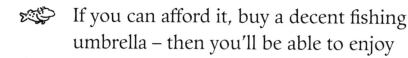 If you can afford it, buy a decent fishing umbrella – then you'll be able to enjoy that summer downpour

Wear a lifejacket when fishing from a boat, even if you can swim

Stay healthy: avoid sewage outflow pipes

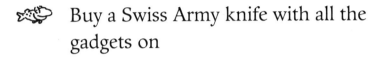 Buy a Swiss Army knife with all the gadgets on

Handle fish with a wet cloth to prevent damaging them

Avoid the perch's dorsal fin...

 ...and the pike's teeth

 Always be prepared to learn a new trick

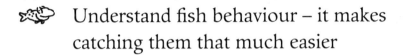 Understand fish behaviour – it makes catching them that much easier

Remember that 10 per cent of the people fishing account for 90 per cent of the fish caught

When you hook a fish, keep the line taut or you may lose it

Don't waste your time fishing once the thermometer climbs above 85 degrees – the fish will stop feeding as the water's oxygen content diminishes

 When in a French restaurant, try fillet of perch. It's a great delicacy

 Make your own flies

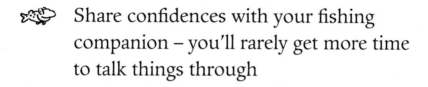 Share confidences with your fishing companion – you'll rarely get more time to talk things through

Foul hooking doesn't count

Occasionally, appreciate the joy of just sitting there, doing nothing

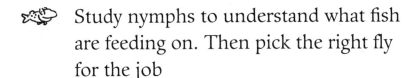 Study nymphs to understand what fish are feeding on. Then pick the right fly for the job

If you are learning to fly-fish, start by casting upstream. That way you will be able to control your line more easily

When lake fishing, use a sliding float where the depth of the water is appreciably greater than the length of your rod. It makes for much easier casting

 Join an angling club to learn a great deal and meet new people

If you need a creative solution to a business problem, try fishing on your own – it will open up the right side of your brain...

 ...but also fish with business associates – they'll become friends

If fishing in North America, learn
to recognize bear prints

 It is possible to combine a family picnic
with a fishing expedition, but make sure
someone is watching the children

Don't walk across private land – you might end up in deep water

 When canal fishing, fish about five feet from the bank – that's often where the fish are

Learn to recognize birdsong

 Carry pocket binoculars with you to appreciate the wildlife fully

 Revel in your surroundings

Recognize when your love of fishing is turning into an obsession...and do something about it. Remember, family first, fishing second

 Don't fish on private waters

Bring a surprise treat for your fishing
companion. Chocolate and a flask of
real coffee is a good start

 Watch *Screaming Reels* on Channel 4
for an entertaining education

At a new venue, get to where you think you want to fish, then walk on for five minutes (Only do this once.)

 It's only a sport, so don't lose your sense of humour

Fish in your local park. You might not catch much, but at five in the morning you'll see it in a completely different light

 If you are fishing and drinking, don't drive

For the ultimate fishing challenge,
go after the Mahseer in India

 Read *Somewhere Down the Crazy River*
by Paul Boot and Jeremy Wade

Try fishing for compliments

 For the full fishing experience, walk into the hills with your camping gear, your oldest friend and a map

 Don't pee into rivers, especially in South America (read Redmond O'Hanlon's *Into the Heart of Borneo* for full explanation)

Remember, there are only three sizes of fish: 'at least five pounds', 'well into double figures' and 'this big' (stand with arms wide apart and tell them that you forgot to take your camera)

 The early bird bags the best fishing spot

Remember that in angling terms, one pound equals eight ounces, and one foot is composed of six inches

 Don't hang a 'Gone fishin' ' sign on the door of your house, unless you really mean 'Burglars welcome'

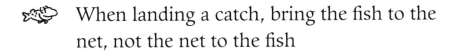 When landing a catch, bring the fish to the net, not the net to the fish

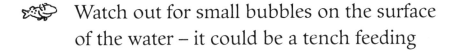 Watch out for small bubbles on the surface of the water – it could be a tench feeding

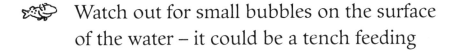 The one that fought and fought is worth a bag full of fish

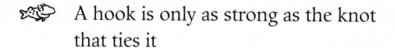 A hook is only as strong as the knot that ties it

A man staring blankly into a lake isn't dead, he's a carp fisherman

Aniseed is good for roach and bad for onlookers

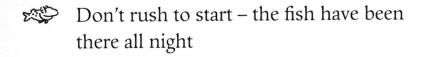 Don't rush to start – the fish have been there all night

The most enjoyable thing about fishing is saying how big it was

The worst thing to catch when fishing is a cold

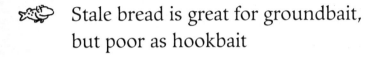 Stale bread is great for groundbait,
but poor as hookbait

East is least and west is best

The maggot that splits is probably dead

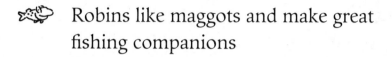 Robins like maggots and make great fishing companions

To get rid of annoying surface feeders like bleak, throw in slices of bread to drift downstream with the current

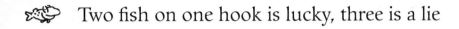 Two fish on one hook is lucky, three is a lie

Wasp grubs are a deadly bait for chub

When fishing near weed use strong line – you don't want to be broken by a fish running for cover

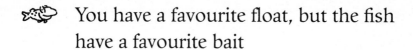 You have a favourite float, but the fish
have a favourite bait

Alter the amount of water in your mix
to affect the way the groundbait sinks –
dropping like a stone or spreading like
a cloud

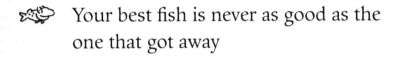 Your best fish is never as good as the one that got away

Adding a small amount of hookbait to your groundbait will educate fish to take the hook

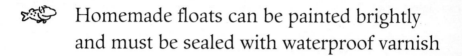 Homemade floats can be painted brightly and must be sealed with waterproof varnish

Experiment with what you add to the groundbait – anything that is edible can attract fish

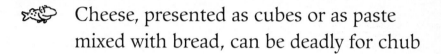 Cheese, presented as cubes or as paste mixed with bread, can be deadly for chub

Small children splashing around in your swim signal it's time to go home

Bright yellow topped floats are less visible than red ones

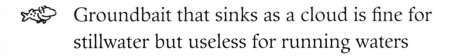 Groundbait that sinks as a cloud is fine for stillwater but useless for running waters

Use nets (landing and keep) without knotted netting as these do less damage to the fish

The most annoying thing about fishing is having to say you caught nothing...

 ...but discovering that your fishing companion couldn't get out of bed runs a pretty close second

Keep your fingers: for pike and other sharp-toothed fish, forceps are needed to remove the hooks and a gag, blunted with corks, is used to hold the fish's mouth open

 Casting into the wind is often pointless; casting with it can add yards to your distance

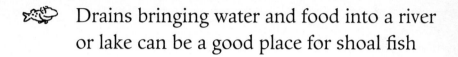 Drains bringing water and food into a river or lake can be a good place for shoal fish

Fishing at the back end of a canal boat can be good and does often come with free drinks

If a heron moves into your patch, move out

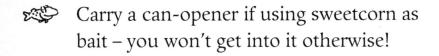 Carry a can-opener if using sweetcorn as bait – you won't get into it otherwise!

Take a dog along for companionship – but make sure it's afraid of water

A bunch of maggots on a 12 to 8 can be irresistible to bream

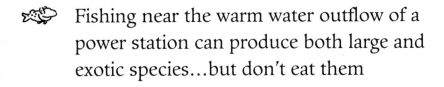 Fishing near the warm water outflow of a power station can produce both large and exotic species...but don't eat them

Fishing next to a pub has many dividends, but be wary, the landlord's heard it all before

If you're sitting right on the water's edge, take care when large boats pass – the resulting wash can wipe out your dry patch!

 If your float shows a bite at the same point every time in your swim, it's a snag on the river bed not a persistent fish

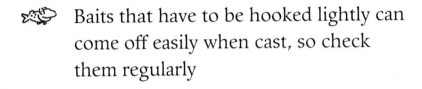 Baits that have to be hooked lightly can come off easily when cast, so check them regularly

Bread flake should be moulded round the hook, leaving the point protruding, with the top pressed round the shank and knot

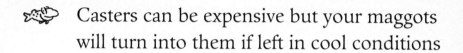 Casters can be expensive but your maggots will turn into them if left in cool conditions

When you've finished with your worms, don't throw them in the water – let them loose on the soil so they can be of use there

Check your bait after a bite to make sure it is still there – maggots can be sucked dry by roach

 Add enough shot to the line to allow the float to cock naturally and not lie too deep

Dog food can be useful carp bait

 Don't use live fish as bait – it's cruel

 New fathers: use a thermometer to test the water temperature, *not* your elbow

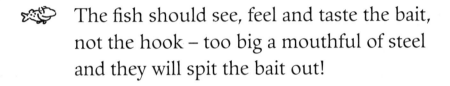 The fish should see, feel and taste the bait, not the hook – too big a mouthful of steel and they will spit the bait out!

Harpooning is inappropriate on most rivers

Use the lightest possible ledger for the conditions – significant resistance on the line might spook the fish

 Use a rod rest to prevent an aching arm – or two if you want a snooze

Look on the bright side: a pleasure boat crossing your swim might actually *encourage* the fish to start feeding by stirring up the bottom and with it any potential food...

 ...but if in any doubt, shower the invading craft with maggots launched from a catapult

Of further interest…

The Traveller's Little Instruction Book
Jo Kyle and Meg Slyfield

As the holidays approach and the level of anxiety rises to fever pitch, reach for this essential guide. Packed full of humorous tips and advice, *The Traveller's Little Instruction Book* will ease away the stress of travelling and provide you with good advice and lashings of wit. Whether you are a student backpacker on a budget, a family on a beach holiday or a professional on a business trip, this is a must.

- It's not a good idea to take sick leave and spend it on the beach in the Caribbean.
- If a sunbronzed god/goddess offers to oil your back, don't argue, just make sure you've got a full bottle.
- If you must relieve yourself in the sea, have the grace to swim around a bit.
- Don't share a one-man tent with a flatulent friend.

The Gardener's Little Instruction Book
Violet Wood

As gardening is the UK's number one hobby, this book will be widely appreciated.

- Plant a buddleia and watch the butterflies dance.
- Don't throw snails over the garden wall.
- Weeding is one of life's therapies.
- Be generous with your cuttings.
- If a plant looks dead, give it the benefit of the doubt.

The Scot's Little Instruction Book

Tony Sweeney

The ideal gift for Scots everywhere.

- Never read the recipe for haggis.
- Don't wear a Celtic strip near an Orange walk.
- Always insist on value for money.
- Don't confuse a Highland fling with a dirty weekend in Inverness.
- Learn key swear words in Gaelic.
- Adopt a canny attitude – don't buy what you canny afford.

The Driver's Little Instruction Book
Mike Leonard

- Don't buy a car just because you like the TV advert.
- When you borrow Dad's car, don't change all his pre-set radio channels.
- Don't try sex in an M.G. Midget unless you have the agility of a gymnast.
- At least once in your life, borrow a soft-top and go for a picnic.
- Don't call the traffic policeman 'son' just because he looks as young as yours.

THE TRAVELLER'S LITTLE INSTRUCTION BOOK	0 7225 3235 0	£3.99	☐
THE GARDENER'S LITTLE INSTRUCTION BOOK	0 7225 3286 5	£3.99	☐
THE SCOT'S LITTLE INSTRUCTION BOOK	0 7225 3328 4	£3.99	☐
THE DRIVER'S LITTLE INSTRUCTION BOOK	0 7225 3163 X	£3.99	☐

All these books are available from your local bookseller or can be ordered direct from the publishers.

To order direct just tick the titles you want and fill in the form below:

Name:
Address:

Postcode:

Send to Thorsons Mail Order, Dept 3, HarperCollins*Publishers*, Westerhill Road, Bishopbriggs, Glasgow G64 2QT.

Please enclose a cheque or postal order or your authority to debit your Visa/Access account —

Credit card no:
Expiry date:
Signature.

— up to the value of the cover price plus:
UK & BFPO: Add £1.00 for the first book and 25p for each additional book ordered.
Overseas orders including Eire: Please add £2.95 service charge. Books will be sent by surface mail but quotes for airmail dispatches will be given on request.
**24-HOUR TELEPHONE ORDERING SERVICE FOR ACCESS/VISA CARDHOLDERS —
TEL: 0141 772 2281.**